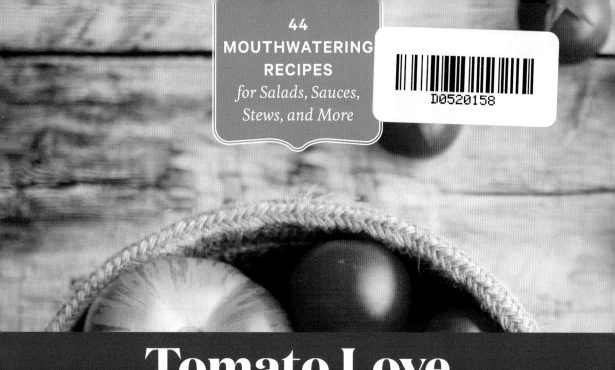

44 MOUTHWATERING RECIPES
for Salads, Sauces, Stews, and More

Tomato Love

Joy Howard

Storey Publishing

To Sandra Jean Lowe, who taught me most of what I know about cooking and everything I know about life

The mission of Storey Publishing is to serve our customers by publishing practical information that encourages personal independence in harmony with the environment.

Edited by Deanna F. Cook and Sarah Guare
Art direction and book design by Michaela Jebb
Text production by Liseann Karandisecky
Indexed by Christine R. Lindemer, Boston Road Communications
Cover and interior photography by © Joe St. Pierre
Additional photography by Zoe Schaeffer/Unsplash, iv; © Erik Gonzalez/Dreamstime.com, i
Photo styling by Ann Lewis
Food styling by Joy Howard

Storey books are available at special discounts when purchased in bulk for premiums and sales promotions as well as for fund-raising or educational use. Special editions or book excerpts can also be created to specification. For details, please call 800-827-8673, or send an email to sales@storey.com.

Storey Publishing
210 MASS MoCA Way
North Adams, MA 01247
storey.com

Printed in the United States by Versa Press
10 9 8 7 6 5 4 3 2 1

Library of Congress Cataloging-in-Publication Data on file

Contents

INTRODUCTION

Tomatoes are the most popular fruit in the world. Yes, fruit. Even the fact that most of us know and use them as a vegetable is a nod to their versatility and alluring complexity. There are literally thousands of varieties of tomatoes, and their diversity in flesh, flavor, size, and color articulate a range that's unmatched by most other fruit. I've yet to try one I didn't love—from the sweet, firm flesh of cherry tomatoes to the musky, meaty richness of many heirlooms.

When I first started conceiving my recipes, I realized how I—and probably most of us, really—rely heavily on tomatoes in the kitchen. They can do the work of saucing, fortifying, or perking up meals any time of day. They're the centerpiece of innumerable versions of pizza (yes!) and pasta (yum!), not to mention all the soups, stews, and salads. My go-to Any-Day Red Sauce (page 95) is one I rely on often, especially on those I-don't-know-what-to-make kinds of nights. A can of plum tomatoes has saved my dinners more times than I'm able to count.

Speaking of cans, eating tomatoes isn't just about the fresh ones that arrive in late summer. Farmers' market fruit is obviously unmatched. But living in New England, that's not how I eat them most often, and I'm guessing many others don't either. We enjoy so many dishes that involve tomatoes year-round that I wanted to make a book that reflected reality, from the sunnier months all the way through the overcast days when your best bet is something you can grab from the shelf and put in a bag. There are recipes here that take advantage of and acknowledge all the ways we eat for real, including delicious tomato products that have an extended shelf life. Yes, I'm talking canned tomatoes, sun-dried tomatoes, tomato paste, and even ketchup. All of them can lend great umami flavor.

I've included many classic dishes, but this book is definitely not a comprehensive collection. Instead, I hope it provides you with the sort of practical, (mostly) everyday recipes you can and will want to return to again and again. I encourage you to try, tweak, and just generally be inspired by the recipes in this book, which include some of my all-time favorites as well as some newer ones. Now get cooking!

Tomato Varieties

You could fill an entire book just listing all the varieties of tomatoes, so I've narrowed it down to the ones I use in this book and what you're likely to find in the grocery store. Obviously, the best fresh fruit will always be whatever you can get your hands on locally in season, but this list takes into account that late summer doesn't last forever!

BEEFSTEAK

A large, bulbous, mildly flavored, and meaty tomato that's great for slicing, sandwich making, and unadulterated eating. Off-season they can be mealy or mushy, so don't bother with these outside of summer.

CAMPARI

Larger than a grape or cherry tomato but still on the smaller side, Camparis are sweet, fleshy, and well suited for all sorts of dishes. You should be able to find them nearly year-round at the grocery store, and the flavor is somewhat reliable even in cooler months. Their larger cousins, "tomatoes on the vine"—the perfectly shaped, ruby red tomatoes sold in clusters of three or more—are also perpetually available and offer similar traits.

CHERRY AND GRAPE

Cooks often use these interchangeably since they're similar in size, but there are some differences. Cherry tomatoes are tiny globe-shaped fruit and tend to be super sweet. Grape tomatoes are also quite small, but they have a more elongated shape and balanced flavor that's as much tomatoey as it is sweet. Grape tomatoes tend to be easier to find off-season. Both varieties have a similarly firm flesh and work well in raw and cooked dishes.

HEIRLOOM

It's not fair to lump the many, many varieties of heirloom tomatoes into one category, but here we are! For the purposes of this book, this category refers to any of the incredibly tasty, often gnarly looking or otherwise uniquely shaped and/or colored fruit that you find at the farmers' market during late summer. They're not great for everything, but boy are they delicious! Use them raw or cooked.

ROMA

Perhaps the most ubiquitous of all grocery store tomatoes, Romas (also known as Italian plum tomatoes) are the long, medium-size fruit you see overflowing in the produce section. They are a favorite variety for canning due to their shape and have a meaty flesh and nice amount of flavor. Like other varieties, they're versatile, but I like them most in recipes that call for chopped tomatoes since they don't have many seeds. But beware—out of season, they can often be mealy or bland.

Cooking with Fresh Tomatoes

There are few foods worse than a tasteless tomato! The best way to avoid less-than-desirable fruit is to stick to buying them fresh in season or opting for conventional varieties known for their consistent sweetness and flavor (looking at you, Campari!). But like anything in nature, there are no guarantees. Here's how to choose the best.

- Look for blemish-free skin with no cracks or punctures.

- The fruit should be heavy for its size and have a fragrant scent.

- If purchasing tomatoes on the vine, the leaves and vine of the fruit should appear fresh and still have a deep green color.

STORING

In general, tomatoes shouldn't be put in the refrigerator—especially if they're still ripening. Most fruit should be left on the counter out of direct sun, ideally in an environment that's not too hot. If your tomatoes are already ripe and you'd like to save them for an extra day or two, put them in the fridge to slow the ripening process.

PREPPING

You're likely well practiced in chopping and slicing, but there are a few other prep techniques that pop up in this book.

Squeeze and chop. I like to use this method for smaller varieties (like cherry, grape, and Campari) that would otherwise be difficult to seed and core with a tool. To do it, gently squeeze the fruit over a sink or bowl to push out the seeds, then chop as desired. There's no need to trim an end of the fruit beforehand.

Seed and core. Tomato seeds have a distinct bitter flavor. They can be tasty, but they're not a good match for every recipe. To remove them, slice the fruit in half or into quarters and trim or scoop away the seeds, pulp, and tough core. A small measuring spoon works well for scraping away seeds that are hard to reach.

Grate. This method comes in handy when you're trying to make a saucy dish or coax the juiciness out of fresh fruit. To do it, trim the stem end of a medium or large tomato. Working over a bowl, use the large holes of a box grater to grate the fruit. Most of the skin will remain intact and can be tossed.

Wedge. This cut works well for salads and other composed dishes. To do it, trim away the stem end of the fruit, if needed (I usually trim and core tomatoes only if they're large). Halve the fruit lengthwise. Lay one half cut-side down on your cutting board and slice the fruit lengthwise into wedges.

Cooking with Pantry Tomatoes

There's no shame in using canned tomatoes, and depending on the time of year, they may be your best bet. Personally, I prefer them over fresh for some recipes like the Any-Day Red Sauce (page 95) because their flavor and quality are always consistent—welcome traits in any ingredient. When it comes to choosing the best canned tomatoes, whole ones are always the way to go (more on that below).

In addition to canned whole tomatoes, there are lots of tomato products that offer both reliability and convenience. The Sweet, Spicy, Smoky Barbecue Sauce (page 96) starts with ketchup, as does the tastiest barbecue sauce I've ever eaten (shout-out to you, Mom!). And both tomato paste and sun-dried tomatoes are easy shortcuts for adding deep tomato flavor to all sorts of dishes.

Not every pantry item is the same, though, and it's not just about quality. Ingredients like herbs, salt, spices, and sugar—just to name a few—can vary greatly from brand to brand and change the taste of a given product as well as your final dish. I have listed some of my own favorites here. Recognizing that tastes can be subjective, you should experiment with different brands and ingredients to see which ones you like best.

CANNED, BOXED, OR BOTTLED TOMATOES

I like to start with whole tomatoes no matter what I'm making. You will not find any recipes here that call for packaged, prechopped tomatoes. That's because most of those commercial products contain chemicals that allow the tomatoes to hold their shape even after they've been cooked. They won't break down well, and the additives make for an inferior-tasting product. Trust me on this! Always use whole tomatoes and chop or purée them as needed. In addition, always read the labels carefully to make sure you're not purchasing ones that have added ingredients like basil, garlic, or tons of salt—a frustrating discovery I've made many times in the middle of cooking! I like San Merican Tomato (S.M.T.) whole peeled tomatoes best.

KETCHUP

Aside from canned tomatoes, this is the one tomato product I feel most strongly about in terms of brand. I prefer Heinz Tomato Ketchup because it's got a nice balance of acid and sweetness, a smooth texture, and, in my opinion, it tastes the most ketchup-y, which is what you really want, right? I like to use it as a base for barbecue sauce and, of course, as a condiment alongside a basket of hot, salty fries.

TOMATO PASTE

You can use this to give your dishes more depth and umami flavor. It's also a great emulsifier, which makes it a surprisingly tasty addition to salad dressing (check out the Southwest Quinoa Salad on page 33). Purchase it in cans so you can easily portion and freeze it. To do so, scoop tablespoon-size mounds onto a parchment paper–lined baking sheet or plate and freeze. Once solid, you can put them in a ziplock freezer bag to keep for months and remove them one at a time as needed. Voilà! No wasted tomato paste.

SUN-DRIED TOMATOES

There's a whole bunch of flavor packed in sun-dried tomatoes, and a little goes a very, very long way. They can be purchased dry or packed in oil. Both are good, but the latter will save you some time in rehydrating, and depending on the brand, it might also mean a little extra flavor from herbs, garlic, and/or spices added to the jar. What's more, you can use the flavorful oil they're packed in as part of your cooking. Purchase the highest-quality halved (not chopped or sliced) ones you can find.

Shakshuka with Extra Vegetables

MAKES 4 SERVINGS

- 3 tablespoons extra-virgin olive oil
- 1 large red bell pepper, chopped
- 1 large yellow onion, chopped
- 3 garlic cloves, minced
- 2½ teaspoons smoked paprika
- 1½ teaspoons ground cumin
- 1¼ teaspoons kosher salt
- ½ teaspoon freshly ground black pepper
- 1 (15-ounce) can chickpeas, drained and rinsed
- ½ small bunch Lacinato kale, ribs removed, chopped
- ¼ cup packed chopped fresh mint
- 1 (28-ounce) can whole tomatoes
- 4 eggs
- ¼ cup crumbled feta cheese
- 2 tablespoons packed chopped fresh parsley
- Pita or sliced hearty bread, for serving

There are so many good things about this North African dish, not the least of which is its versatility. The poached eggs give it a breakfast-y feel, while its savory, herbaceous tomato sauce makes it a strong dinnertime contender (at my house we serve it both ways). For this version I added chickpeas and kale to make it a more filling main. After you've scooped the eggs onto plates, bring the pan to the table to enjoy what's left over family-style, with lots of extra bread.

1. Heat the oil in a 9- or 10-inch cast-iron skillet over medium-high heat. Add the bell pepper and onion, and cook, undisturbed, until beginning to brown, about 5 minutes. Reduce the heat to medium-low and cook, stirring occasionally, until the pepper is soft, about 3 minutes longer.

2. Stir in the garlic and cook for 1 minute. Add the paprika, cumin, salt, and black pepper, and cook until fragrant, 1 minute. Stir in the chickpeas, kale, and 2 tablespoons of the mint, and cook until the kale is wilted, about 3 minutes. Use your hands to break the tomatoes into small pieces and add them, along with their juices, to the skillet. Continue to cook, stirring occasionally, until the sauce has thickened slightly, about 10 minutes.

3. Make a well along the side of the pan and crack an egg into it. Repeat, making three more wells and cracking an egg into each. Reduce the heat to low, cover, and cook until the eggs are set, about 10 minutes.

4. Top with the feta, parsley, and remaining 2 tablespoons mint. Serve immediately with pita or sliced bread.

Ham and Egg Breakfast Cups

MAKES 12 BREAKFAST CUPS

Cooking spray

12 large slices Black Forest ham (from a deli counter)

1½ cups shredded cheddar cheese

1 cup quartered cherry tomatoes

12 eggs

Kosher salt and freshly ground black pepper

4 teaspoons chopped fresh chives, for garnish

Push past the packaged stuff and go straight to the deli counter when you're choosing the ham for this recipe. The reason is the size: As the slices cook, they shrink significantly, and you'll need ones that hang over the edge. Most presliced meats don't make the cut.

1. Preheat the oven to 400°F (200°C). Coat a standard-size muffin pan with cooking spray.

2. Press a slice of ham into each well to form a cup, letting the excess hang over the sides (it will shrink as it cooks). Add 1 tablespoon of the cheese to each cup.

3. Set aside ⅓ cup of the tomatoes. Evenly divide the remaining ⅔ cup tomatoes among the muffin wells and crack an egg into each well.

4. Bake the eggs for about 15 minutes, or until set. Let the cups cool in the pan for 5 minutes, then use a silicone spatula to remove them from the wells. Season with salt and pepper. To serve, garnish each cup with some of the reserved tomatoes and the chives.

Mushroom, Kale, and Tomato Strata

MAKES 12 SERVINGS

- 8 cups cubed whole-grain bread
- 1 tablespoon extra-virgin olive oil
- 2 garlic cloves, minced
- 8 ounces white mushrooms, sliced
- 1 small bunch green curly kale, ribs removed and leaves torn into bite-size pieces
- 1¼ teaspoons kosher salt
- ¾ teaspoon freshly ground black pepper
- 1½ cups shredded Gruyère cheese
- ¾ cup shredded sharp cheddar cheese
- 1 tablespoon unsalted butter, for greasing the pan
- 1 cup halved cherry or grape tomatoes
- 8 eggs
- 2 cups whole milk

Though it's more eggy than a bread pudding, a strata starts with the same rich, carb-filled goodness. Far from a light dish, it's not the kind of thing you'd want to eat every day, but it is the kind of thing that makes for a great brunch when you want to win over your friends with food. An added bonus: You can assemble it a day ahead.

1. Preheat the oven to 400°F (200°C).

2. Spread the bread onto a baking sheet and toast in the oven for about 8 minutes, or until dried out and lightly crisped. Reduce the oven to 350°F (180°C).

3. Warm the oil in a large skillet over medium heat. Add the garlic and cook until fragrant, about 1 minute. Add the mushrooms and cook until they begin to release their juices, about 3 minutes. Stir in the kale, ½ teaspoon of the salt, and ¼ teaspoon of the pepper, and continue to cook, stirring occasionally, until the kale is wilted, about 4 minutes. Remove from the heat.

4. Toss together the Gruyère and cheddar in a small bowl.

5. Coat a 9- by 13-inch baking dish with the butter. Cover the bottom of the dish with one-third of the bread cubes. Sprinkle on one-third each of the mushroom mixture, tomatoes, and cheese. Repeat the layers twice more in this manner, starting with the bread cubes and ending with the cheese.

6. Whisk together the eggs, milk, and the remaining ¾ teaspoon salt and ½ teaspoon pepper in a large bowl. Pour the mixture over the strata, making sure to moisten all the bread. Use a sheet of plastic wrap to gently press the bread into the egg mixture and cover the strata. Let sit for 30 minutes.

7. Bake the strata for about 40 minutes, or until it's set in the center, rotating the pan halfway through. Serve right away.

Sun-Dried Tomato Scones
with Scallion Butter

MAKES 8 SCONES

Scones

- 2 cups all-purpose flour, plus more for dusting
- 1 tablespoon sugar
- 2 teaspoons baking powder
- ½ teaspoon kosher salt
- ½ cup (1 stick) cold unsalted butter
- ½ cup half-and-half
- 1 egg
- ¼ cup oil-packed sun-dried tomatoes, drained and minced
- 1 garlic clove, grated

Scallion Butter

- 1 scallion, minced
- 6 tablespoons unsalted butter, softened
- ⅛ teaspoon kosher salt

Cold butter and a pastry blender do the trick when it comes to making perfectly flaky scones, but using a pastry blender can be a bit tedious. Instead, this recipe uses a grater. It's a far simpler and more streamlined method for achieving bakery-worthy texture. I don't remember whom I should thank for this baking hack, but I'll never go back to the old method.

1. To make the scones, stir together the flour, sugar, baking powder, and salt in a large bowl. Use the large holes of a box grater to grate the butter into the flour mixture. Use your hands to toss the butter into the flour occasionally as you shred.

2. In another bowl, whisk together the half-and-half, egg, tomatoes, and garlic. Combine with the flour mixture until the flour is moistened. Do not overmix.

3. Line a baking sheet with parchment paper. Turn out the dough onto a lightly floured surface and pat into a ½-inch-thick circle. Slice the round into eight wedges and transfer the scones to the prepared baking sheet. Place in the freezer and leave there while the oven preheats.

4. Preheat the oven to 400°F (200°C).

5. Bake the scones for 20 to 25 minutes, or until golden brown on the top and bottom, rotating the pan halfway through.

6. While the scones cool briefly, make the scallion butter: Stir together the scallion, butter, and salt in a small bowl. Serve with the warm scones.

Tomato–Goat Cheese Tart

MAKES 8 SERVINGS

1½ pounds mixed tomatoes, halved if small, or cut into wedges if larger

1½ teaspoons herbes de Provence

½ teaspoon kosher salt

¼ teaspoon freshly ground black pepper

Rolled pie dough for a single-crust 9-inch pie

1 tablespoon unsalted butter

1 tablespoon extra-virgin olive oil

4 large shallots, sliced

1 tablespoon plus 2 teaspoons Dijon mustard

2 ounces goat cheese, crumbled

A buttery, flaky pastry crust filled with freshly picked fruit or vegetables is just the kind of cooking I crave during the summer months: effortless prep and minimal ingredients that let the produce shine. This tart is based on a classic French recipe that includes herbes de Provence and Dijon mustard, but tomatoes are the real star, so aim to work with the very best ones you can get your hands on. Extra points if you grew them yourself or they're from a farm share.

1. Preheat the oven to 400°F (200°C).

2. Toss together the tomatoes, herbes de Provence, ½ teaspoon of the salt, and the pepper in a colander. Let sit for 30 minutes.

3. Meanwhile, press the pie dough into a 9-inch tart pan and trim away the excess. Freeze 10 minutes. Line the dough with parchment paper and fill it with dried beans or pie weights. Bake for about 10 minutes, or until the crust begins to turn golden around the edges. Remove the weights and parchment, then bake for 5 minutes longer. Remove the crust from the oven, then increase the oven temperature to 425°F (220°C).

4. While the crust bakes, warm the butter with the oil in a medium skillet over medium heat until the butter is melted. Add the shallots and cook until they've softened and browned, about 5 minutes.

5. Spread the mustard over the bottom of the par-baked crust. Scatter on the shallots. Use a paper towel to lightly pat dry the tomatoes, then arrange them atop the shallots. Sprinkle with the goat cheese.

6. Bake for about 40 minutes, or until the tomatoes are tender and brown in spots and the piecrust is golden brown, rotating the pan once halfway through. Let cool for 10 minutes before serving.

Herb, Egg, and Tomato Scramble

MAKES 2 SERVINGS

4 eggs

2 tablespoons chopped fresh herbs (I prefer equal parts dill, basil, and cilantro)

¼ teaspoon kosher salt

Freshly ground black pepper

2 teaspoons unsalted butter

8 cherry tomatoes, squeezed and roughly chopped

This recipe was inspired by a breakfast served at a café called Haymarket in Northampton, Massachusetts, where my husband and I spent many Saturday mornings with our daughters when they were little. It's a homey place, with no airs, a strong sense of community, and a great breakfast called Herbs and Eggs. The dish is as simple as the name sounds, but don't let that fool you— herbs and eggs are an addictive combination. Adding tomatoes to the scramble takes it to the next level.

1. Whisk together the eggs, herbs, salt, and a grind or two of pepper in a small bowl.

2. Melt the butter in a small skillet over medium heat. Add the egg mixture and cook until it begins to set. With a silicone spatula, gently lift and fold the mixture as it cooks to form large curds. Just before the scramble has reached the desired consistency, fold in the tomatoes. Cook for a few seconds longer, then evenly divide between two plates and serve immediately.

Pan con Tomate

MAKES 4 SERVINGS

- ½ loaf ciabatta, halved crosswise and cut into 2-inch-wide slices
- 1 tablespoon extra-virgin olive oil, plus more for drizzling
- 2 medium-size heirloom tomatoes
- 1 large garlic clove, peeled

  Flaky salt
- 2 ounces Manchego cheese, shaved (optional)

Assembled with few ingredients, this Spanish tapa, whose name translates as "bread with tomato," hardly warrants a recipe, but its delicious simplicity makes it worth a mention. Typically, grilled or toasted bread is served with whole pieces of tomato so that diners can rub the freshly cut fruit onto the bread themselves. This version uses grated tomatoes, and the juicy pulp gets spooned onto the bread with the same irresistible results.

1. Preheat the broiler. Place the bread on a baking sheet and brush with the oil. Toast for 1 to 2 minutes, or until dark brown in spots.

2. Trim the stem end from each tomato. Use the large holes of a box grater to grate each tomato, cut-side down, over a bowl. Discard the skin.

3. Rub each toast slice with the garlic and top with a few spoonfuls of grated tomato. Arrange the toasts on a platter, drizzle with oil, and sprinkle generously with salt. Scatter on the cheese, if using. Serve immediately.

Caramelized Onion and Tomato Jam

MAKES 1 CUP

- ¾ teaspoon cumin seeds
- ½ teaspoon coriander seeds
- ½ teaspoon fennel seeds
- 2 tablespoons canola oil
- 2 teaspoons grated fresh ginger
- 2 medium yellow onions, chopped
- 2 teaspoons kosher salt
- ¼ teaspoon red pepper flakes
- ¼ cup apple cider vinegar
- 1½ pounds Roma tomatoes, seeded, cored, and cut into ½-inch dice
- ⅓ cup firmly packed dark brown sugar
- Crackers or toasted baguette, for serving

A combination of aromatic cumin, coriander, and fennel seeds along with fresh ginger give this savory-sweet spread its warm, earthy flavor that's a subtle nod to South Asian cooking. The onions are first caramelized, then cooked low and slow with tomatoes until they break down into a dark, sticky jam. Eat it with crackers or a baguette, or use it to top a burger.

1. Use a spice grinder or a mortar and pestle to crush the cumin, coriander, and fennel seeds into a powder. Heat the oil in a large heavy pot over medium-high heat. Fry the spices for 1 minute, then add the ginger and cook for 30 seconds.

2. Add the onions, salt, and pepper flakes, and sauté, stirring frequently and scraping the bottom of the pot, until the onions are golden and caramelized, about 25 minutes. If needed, splash in water, 1 tablespoon at a time, to prevent burning.

3. Add the vinegar and scrape up the browned bits from the bottom of the pan. Stir in the tomatoes and sugar, and bring the mixture to a boil. Reduce the heat to low and simmer until the mixture is thick and jammy, about 40 minutes. Let cool, then refrigerate until ready to use. Serve with crackers or a toasted baguette.

BLTKs

(Bacon, Lettuce, Tomato Kebabs)

MAKES 24 KEBABS

Creamy Chipotle Dip

- ½ cup plain Greek yogurt
- ¼ cup mayonnaise
- 1 chipotle chile (from a can of chipotle chiles in adobo sauce), roughly chopped
- Juice of ½ lime
- 1 garlic clove, grated
- ¼ teaspoon kosher salt
- ¼ teaspoon sweet paprika
- 4 teaspoons minced fresh cilantro

Kebabs

- 24 cherry tomatoes, halved
- 12 strips cooked thick-cut bacon, each broken into 4 pieces
- 3 leaves iceberg or green leaf lettuce, torn into bite-size pieces

It's true, you could just make a sandwich, but these kebabs aren't meant to be a meal. They're something you can casually enjoy with friends or anyone who's patient enough to keep their hands off the bacon while you put these treats together. There's even a spicy chipotle-yogurt dip served on the side. It's a very good, shareable snack. Note that you will need 4-inch toothpicks for this recipe.

1. To make the dip, place the yogurt, mayonnaise, chile, lime juice, garlic, salt, paprika, and cilantro in a small bowl and use an immersion blender to blend. Refrigerate until ready to serve.

2. To assemble each kebab, thread a tomato half, cut-side up, onto a toothpick. Stack 2 bacon pieces and a few lettuce pieces on top, then thread on another tomato half cut-side down. Place on a platter or plate. Repeat with the remaining ingredients. Serve the kebabs with the dip on the side.

Tomato Grilled Cheese

MAKES 2 SANDWICHES

- 1 cup shredded sharp cheddar cheese
- ⅓ cup shredded Gruyère cheese
- 2–3 tablespoons mayonnaise
- 4 slices hearty sourdough bread
- 1 medium or large heirloom tomato, sliced

Just like peanut butter and jelly or tuna and mayo, tomatoes and melty cheese are a combination that's meant to be. It's a heavenly match (in this case, cheddar, Gruyère, and heirlooms) that's made even better by using mayonnaise in place of butter to get the bread golden and crunchy. If you prefer a hearty bakery bread to standard sandwich slices, you may need a little more cheese and mayo than what the recipe calls for. Adjust accordingly, and don't sweat it. This sandwich is hard to mess up.

1. Toss together the cheeses in a small bowl. Spread a thin layer of mayonnaise onto one side of each bread slice. Flip two of the slices over and sprinkle each with one-quarter of the cheese. Layer each with half the tomatoes and top each with one-quarter of the cheese and another slice of bread, mayo-side up.

2. Warm a large skillet over medium-low heat. Place each sandwich in the skillet and toast until golden brown, about 4 minutes. Flip and brown on the other side, about 3 minutes. Serve immediately.

Sun-Dried Tomato–White Bean Dip

MAKES ABOUT 2 CUPS

- 1 (15-ounce) can great Northern beans, rinsed and drained
- ¼ cup lemon juice (from about 1½ lemons)
- ¼ cup plus 1 tablespoon oil-packed sun-dried tomatoes, drained and chopped
- ¼ cup tahini
- ¼ cup extra-virgin olive oil, plus more for garnish
- 3 tablespoons water, plus more as needed
- 1 garlic clove, chopped
- ¾ teaspoon smoked paprika, plus more for garnish
- 1 teaspoon kosher salt
- ¼ teaspoon freshly ground black pepper
- 2 tablespoons chopped parsley leaves, for garnish
- Sliced vegetables and crackers or baguette, for serving

If you're a fan of hummus, you'll appreciate this riff on the classic dip that features sun-dried tomatoes and a hint of unexpected flavor, thanks to the addition of smoked paprika. Great Northern beans take the place of chickpeas, but the dip has the same rich and creamy texture as its better-known counterpart. Serve it with crackers and fresh veggies or spread it on a sandwich that needs a little extra something.

1. Combine the beans, lemon juice, tomatoes, tahini, oil, water, garlic, paprika, salt, and pepper in a food processor or blender. Purée until smooth. If the mixture is too thick, add more water, 1 tablespoon at a time. Taste and adjust the seasoning if needed.

2. Transfer the dip to a bowl, drizzle with oil, and sprinkle with paprika. Scatter on the parsley. Serve with sliced vegetables and crackers or baguette slices on the side.

Chipotle Salsa

MAKES 2 CUPS

- 1 (14-ounce) can fire-roasted diced tomatoes
- 1 small red onion, roughly chopped
- 1 chipotle chile (from a can of chipotle chiles in adobo sauce)
- Juice of 1 lime
- 2 tablespoons chopped fresh cilantro
- 1 garlic clove, minced
- 1 teaspoon kosher salt
- Tortilla chips, for serving

This restaurant-style salsa starts with tomatoes from a can; the cilantro, onion, lime, and garlic give it bright notes. Using fire-roasted tomatoes enhances the smokiness of the chipotle chile. Think of the recipe as a starting point, then taste and adjust the flavors as needed—add chiles for more heat, cilantro or lime for more zest, or garlic and onion for more dimension. It's great alongside chips, or in the Enchilada Stacks with Chipotle Salsa (page 76).

1. Place the tomatoes and their juice, onion, chile, lime juice, cilantro, garlic, and salt in a food processor and pulse until the desired consistency is reached.

2. Taste and adjust the flavor as desired. Serve with tortilla chips.

Shrimp Cocktail for Two

MAKES 2 SERVINGS

Shrimp

- 3 ribs celery, cut into 3-inch pieces
- 3 bay leaves
- 2 lemons, 1 halved; 1 cut into wedges, for serving
- 1 tablespoon black peppercorns
- ¾ pound large raw shrimp, peeled and deveined

Cocktail Sauce

- ⅔ cup chili sauce (I prefer Heinz)
- 2 tablespoons prepared horseradish
- 1 tablespoon plus 1 teaspoon lemon juice
- 1 teaspoon Tabasco sauce
- ½ teaspoon kosher salt
- ¼ teaspoon freshly ground black pepper

When I was a kid, I thought shrimp cocktail was the fanciest thing you could order at a restaurant. Though years of cooking and eating have proven otherwise, the combination of plump shellfish and spicy-sweet horseradish-y sauce still brings me the same amount of delight. But please, do not overcook the shrimp! Once they're pink and opaque they are done; if they're curled into a tight "O" shape, they'll be rubbery. You want a nice, curved "C" shape perfect for hanging on a cocktail glass, just as my 8-year-old self would have loved.

1. To make the shrimp, fill a large pot with 3 quarts of water. Add the celery, bay leaves, lemon halves, and peppercorns. Bring to a boil. Remove from the heat, then add the shrimp and let sit until no longer pink, about 3 minutes.

2. While the shrimp cooks, prepare an ice bath. Once the shrimp is done, transfer it to the ice bath to stop the cooking. Strain out the shrimp, pat dry, and transfer to a platter. Refrigerate until ready to serve.

3. To make the cocktail sauce, stir together the chili sauce, horseradish, lemon juice, Tabasco, salt, and pepper in a small bowl. Taste and adjust the flavor as desired.

4. Serve the shrimp with cocktail sauce and the lemon wedges on the side.

7/17/22
very good

Southwest Quinoa Salad

MAKES 6-8 SERVINGS

Dressing

Juice of 1 lime

1 tablespoon tomato paste

1 garlic clove, grated

1/2 t ¾ teaspoon kosher salt

½ teaspoon smoked paprika

⅛ teaspoon chipotle chili powder

¼ cup plus 2 tablespoons extra-virgin olive oil

Salad

1 cup canned black beans, rinsed and drained

1 cup halved cherry or grape tomatoes

¾ cup frozen corn, thawed

¼ cup finely chopped red onion

½ small red bell pepper, chopped

½ small yellow bell pepper, chopped

3 cups cooked quinoa, chilled

1 avocado, diced

¼ cup crumbled queso fresco

¼ cup roughly chopped fresh cilantro

To make a really good vinaigrette, you need an emulsifier—something that keeps the oil and vinegar (or in this case, lime juice) from separating and gives the dressing a smooth, almost creamy texture. Here, tomato paste does the trick. In addition to making the dressing for this recipe extra tomatoey, it helps bring together all the other flavors. Don't skip letting the quinoa cool completely before you dress the salad, or it will end up less luscious than intended.

1. To make the dressing, whisk together the lime juice, tomato paste, garlic, salt, paprika, and chili powder in a small bowl. Add the oil in a slow, steady stream, while whisking vigorously until emulsified.

2. To assemble the salad, combine the beans, tomatoes, corn, onion, and bell peppers in a large bowl. Add the quinoa and dressing, then stir to evenly coat. Spread onto a platter and top with the avocado, queso fresco, and cilantro. Keep refrigerated until ready to serve.

Tomato and Peach Panzanella
with Smoked Mozzarella

MAKES 6 SERVINGS

- 2 pita bread rounds, halved and cut into 1-inch-wide strips
- 6 tablespoons extra-virgin olive oil
- Kosher salt
- 3 tablespoons red wine vinegar
- 1½ teaspoons Dijon mustard
- Freshly ground black pepper
- 2 pounds mixed tomatoes (I like to use cherry and small heirlooms), halved or sliced into wedges
- 3 ripe peaches, sliced into wedges
- ¼ cup thinly sliced red onion
- 2 ounces smoked fresh mozzarella, torn into bite-size pieces *white cheddar used w/ smoke*
- ¼ cup finely chopped fresh parsley
- 8 large basil leaves, roughly chopped

Peaches—check! Lots of herbs—check! Carbs—check! A good number of my favorite things are in this salad, including a well-balanced matchup of savory and sweet ingredients. The recipe makes several servings, but if you don't plan to share (no judgment), portion it and add the appropriate amount of bread and dressing only to what you're eating right away. That way you won't end up with sad, soggy bread leftovers.

1. Preheat the oven to 400°F (200°C).

2. Arrange the pita pieces evenly on a baking sheet. Brush them with 1 tablespoon of the oil and season lightly with salt. Bake for about 8 minutes, or until golden, flipping once.

3. Whisk together the vinegar and mustard in a large bowl. Vigorously whisk in the remaining 5 tablespoons oil until emulsified. Season with salt and pepper.

4. Add the tomatoes, peaches, onion, mozzarella, parsley, and basil to the bowl and toss to coat. Break the bread into smaller pieces, scatter them into the bowl, and toss the salad once more. Serve immediately.

Caprese Pasta Salad with Salami

MAKES 6 SERVINGS

- 12 ounces casarecce or gemelli pasta
- 3 tablespoons balsamic vinegar
- 1 small garlic clove, grated
- ¾ teaspoon dried oregano
- ½ teaspoon kosher salt
- ½ teaspoon freshly ground black pepper
- ¼ cup extra-virgin olive oil
- 2 cups cherry tomatoes, halved
- 1 cup fresh mozzarella pearls
- 3 ounces salami, sliced into half-moons
- 12 large basil leaves, roughly chopped, plus more for garnish
- 1 small shallot, sliced
- 2 cups baby arugula

In spite of all the gorgeous produce available, summer is the season when I most often find myself not wanting to cook. (I'd rather be outside!) On those days I'll throw together something like this pasta salad and call it a meal, offering some fresh fruit afterward for good measure. While the tomatoes work nicely with arugula and salami, you can skip the latter to make the salad vegetarian, or add whatever raw summer vegetables you have on hand.

1. Cook the pasta according to the package directions. Drain, rinse with cool water, and set aside.

2. Stir together the vinegar, garlic, oregano, salt, and pepper in a large bowl. Whisk in the oil in a slow, steady stream until emulsified.

3. Add the tomatoes, mozzarella, salami, basil, and shallot, and dressing to the bowl and toss to coat. Add the pasta and arugula and toss once more. Refrigerate until ready to serve. Just before serving, garnish the salad with additional basil.

Wedge Salad

with Baked Summer Tomatoes

MAKES 4 SERVINGS

Dressing

- ½ cup buttermilk
- ¼ cup plus 2 tablespoons extra-virgin olive oil
- ¼ cup plus 2 tablespoons crumbled blue cheese
- 2 tablespoons mayonnaise
- 2 tablespoons sour cream
- Juice of ½ lemon
- 1 garlic clove, chopped
- ½ teaspoon kosher salt
- ¼ teaspoon freshly ground black pepper

Baked Tomatoes

- ½ cup panko breadcrumbs
- 2 tablespoons grated Parmesan cheese
- 2 tablespoons extra-virgin olive oil
- 1 teaspoon lemon zest
- ½ teaspoon kosher salt
- ¼ teaspoon freshly ground black pepper
- 2 ripe medium-size tomatoes, halved crosswise and seeds scooped out

Salad

- 1 small head iceberg lettuce, cut into 4 wedges
- 6 strips cooked bacon, crumbled
- 2 tablespoons chopped fresh chives

With a few small changes, this recipe morphs a standard steakhouse salad into an indulgent main course. Cherry tomatoes—usually scattered over the iceberg—are replaced with larger fruit that's topped with a lemony panko crust, baked, and served on the side. Don't worry: There's still bacon and blue cheese, too.

1. To make the dressing, place the buttermilk, oil, ¼ cup of the blue cheese, the mayonnaise, sour cream, lemon juice, garlic, salt, and pepper in a large cup or jar. Mix with an immersion blender, then stir in the remaining 2 tablespoons blue cheese. Refrigerate until ready to use.

2. Preheat the oven to 425°F (220°C). Line a baking sheet with parchment paper.

3. To make the baked tomatoes, stir together the breadcrumbs, Parmesan, oil, lemon zest, salt, and pepper in a small bowl. Arrange the tomatoes, cut-side up, on the baking sheet. Sprinkle with the breadcrumb mixture. Bake for about 12 minutes, or until the topping is golden brown.

4. To assemble the salad, place each lettuce wedge on a small plate. Drizzle each with 2 or 3 tablespoons of the dressing (refrigerate the rest for later use) and sprinkle with the bacon and chives. Place a tomato on the side of each plate and serve immediately.

Sugar Snap Peas

with High-Summer Tomatoes, Herbs, and Tahini

MAKES 6 SERVINGS

- 3 tablespoons extra-virgin olive oil
- 3 tablespoons tahini
- 2 tablespoons water
- 1 tablespoon plus 2 teaspoons lemon juice
- 1 garlic clove, grated
- ¾ teaspoon kosher salt

  Freshly ground black pepper
- 10 ounces mixed summer tomatoes, halved or sliced into wedges
- 8 ounces sugar snap peas, strings removed, halved
- 3 tablespoons roughly chopped mixed fresh herbs (I like mint, parsley, and basil)

The deep, nutty flavor of toasted sesame seeds is a complement to many dishes, including salads like this one made with sweet sugar snaps and vine-ripened tomatoes. Here the sesame takes the form of tahini, which is used as the base for an addictively tasty four-ingredient dressing with olive oil, lemon, and garlic. Once you've tried it, you'll likely want to drizzle it on everything—and you can. It also works well with falafel, grilled meat, and roasted vegetables.

1. Whisk together the oil, tahini, water, lemon juice, and garlic in a small bowl. Season with the salt and a few grinds of pepper.

2. Combine the tomatoes and peas in a large bowl. Add ¼ cup of the tahini dressing and toss to coat. Transfer to a serving bowl and scatter on the herbs. Serve with extra dressing on the side.

Patlican Soslu

MAKES 8 SERVINGS

- 2 small eggplants (about 1½ pounds), cut into 1-inch cubes

- 1 tablespoon plus 1¼ teaspoons kosher salt

- Canola oil, for frying

- 4 sweet medium-size tomatoes

- 2 tablespoons extra-virgin olive oil, plus more for drizzling

- 1 large cubanelle pepper, chopped

- 3 garlic cloves, chopped

- 2 tablespoons tomato paste

- 2 teaspoons sugar

- ¼ teaspoon red pepper flakes

- Pita bread, for serving

- Chopped fresh parsley, for garnish (optional)

My husband's job has occasionally taken us to Turkey for the summer, and whenever we go, this is the dish I seek out the most. Typically served as a cold starter with bread, it's essentially eggplant (patlican) that's first panfried, then simmered in tomato sauce (soslu). It's not a particularly complicated dish, but that just makes me love it even more. Served along with some wine or a cocktail, it's a great beginning to a meal during the summer months, when you have the chance to use super fresh, in-season produce.

1. Place the eggplant in a colander and sprinkle with 1 tablespoon of the salt. Toss gently, then let sit for 10 minutes. Rinse with cool water, then gently press the eggplant against the sides of the colander to drain any excess liquid. Pat the cubes dry with a tea towel.

2. Line a plate with paper towels. Heat ¾ inch of canola oil in a large high-sided skillet over medium-high heat until it reaches 350°F (177°C). Working in batches, fry the eggplant, turning occasionally, until golden, about 6 minutes per batch. Drain on the paper towel–lined plate.

3. Trim away the stem end of each tomato, then grate into a bowl with a box grater. Discard the skin and set aside.

4. Warm the olive oil in a large skillet over medium heat. Add the cubanelle pepper and sauté until beginning to brown, about 3 minutes. Add the garlic and cook for 1 minute. Stir in the grated tomatoes, tomato paste, sugar, pepper flakes, and remaining 1¼ teaspoons salt. Bring to a simmer. Cook until the mixture begins to thicken and reduce, about 15 minutes.

5. Add the eggplant and continue to simmer to let the flavors meld, about 5 minutes. Let cool completely. Just before serving, drizzle with olive oil. Serve cold or at room temperature with pita. Garnish with parsley, if using.

Spicy Gazpacho

MAKES 4 SERVINGS

- 2 pounds sweet, ripe tomatoes, seeded, cored, and roughly chopped
- ½ English cucumber, roughly chopped
- ½ medium red onion, quartered
- 2 medium ribs celery (from the center of the bunch), roughly chopped
- 1 small red bell pepper, roughly chopped
- 2 garlic cloves, sliced
- 2 tablespoons red wine vinegar
- 1 tablespoon pickled jalapeños
- 2 teaspoons kosher salt
- ½ teaspoon freshly ground black pepper
- 3 tablespoons extra-virgin olive oil, plus more for garnish
- 1 cup cubed hearty white bread (crusts removed)
- Sungold or red cherry tomatoes, halved, for garnish
- Cilantro leaves, for garnish

Heartier versions of gazpacho have their place, but if you haven't made (or eaten) one that's silky smooth, I urge you to give it a try. To achieve the texture, the ingredients are blended together then strained through a sieve, leaving behind all the teensy bits. You'll want the best tomatoes you can find, so if it's not tomato season, save this recipe for later.

1. Toss together the chopped tomatoes, cucumber, onion, celery, bell pepper, garlic, vinegar, jalapeños, salt, and black pepper. Let sit at room temperature for 30 minutes.

2. Place the vegetables in a blender, along with the oil and bread, and purée until smooth. Strain through a sieve and refrigerate until well chilled, about 2 hours. Serve cold. Garnish with cherry tomatoes, more oil, and cilantro.

Roasted Tomato Basil Soup
with Pumpernickel Croutons

MAKES 6 SERVINGS

Croutons

- 3 slices pumpernickel bread, cut into ½-inch cubes
- 1 tablespoon plus 1 teaspoon extra-virgin olive oil
- ½ cup finely grated Parmesan cheese (see note)
- ¼ teaspoon kosher salt

Soup

- 2 tablespoons unsalted butter
- 1 tablespoon extra-virgin olive oil
- 1 large onion, chopped
- 3 large garlic cloves, minced
- ½ teaspoon kosher salt
- ¼ teaspoon freshly ground black pepper
- 1 tablespoon tomato paste
- 3 cups chicken broth
- 2 batches Herb-Roasted Grape Tomatoes (page 91)
- ⅓ cup basil leaves

NOTE: Finely grating the Parmesan with a Microplane will help it adhere to the croutons. If you don't have one, you can wing it by tossing the bread with the cheese as best you can, then sprinkling whatever doesn't stick over the bread before baking.

A bowl of this dinner-worthy, extra herby soup is sure to satisfy. Take note that you'll need a double batch of the Herb-Roasted Grape Tomatoes (page 91) to make this soup. If you're making them just for this recipe, a standard baking sheet can accommodate all you need, but you'll likely have to leave the batch in the oven for a bit longer (all the fruit should be wrinkled, and at least a few should be brown in spots).

1. Preheat the oven to 400°F (200°C). Line a baking sheet with parchment paper.

2. To make the croutons, toss together the bread cubes and oil in a small bowl. Add the Parmesan and toss once more. Spread the croutons onto the prepared baking sheet and sprinkle with any remaining cheese from the bowl. Bake for about 12 minutes, or until crisp. Sprinkle with the salt.

3. Meanwhile, prepare the soup. Melt the butter and warm the oil in a Dutch oven over medium heat. Add the onion and sauté for 3 minutes. Add the garlic, salt, and pepper, and sauté for 1 minute.

4. Stir in the tomato paste and cook, stirring occasionally, until slightly darkened, 2 minutes. Add the broth and tomatoes, and bring to a boil. Lower the heat and simmer until the soup is slightly reduced, about 15 minutes.

5. Add the basil. Purée the soup in the pot with an immersion blender. Serve the soup in bowls, with croutons scattered on top.

Instant Pot Black Lentil Stew

MAKES 8 SERVINGS

- 1 tablespoon extra-virgin olive oil
- 1 pound hot Italian sausage, casings removed
- 1 large onion, chopped
- 4 garlic cloves, minced
- 1 large bunch green kale, ribs removed, chopped (about 8 cups)
- 1¼ teaspoons kosher salt
- ½ teaspoon freshly ground black pepper
- 1 (28-ounce) can whole tomatoes
- 6 cups chicken broth
- 1½ pounds russet potatoes, cut into 1- to 2-inch pieces
- 1⅓ cups black lentils, rinsed and picked over
- Juice of 1 lemon
- 4 sprigs thyme
- 2 sprigs rosemary
- Grated Parmesan cheese, for serving (optional)

If coziness can be delivered by the bowl, this recipe has all the right ingredients: a homey blend of spicy Italian sausage, lentils, greens, rosemary, and a bright note of citrus. (And did I mention the potatoes?) They all come together in a stew that's hearty but not too heavy—just the kind of dish you want on a chilly winter day. After just a few minutes of tending to the pot, you can snuggle under a blanket while your pressure cooker does the rest of the work.

1. Set an electric pressure cooker to sauté and warm the oil. Line a plate with paper towels. Cook the sausage in the pot until browned, about 5 minutes, then transfer to the prepared plate.

2. Spoon all but 1 tablespoon of oil from the pot. Add the onion and cook until softened, about 3 minutes. Add the garlic and cook for 1 minute. Stir in the kale, salt, and pepper, and cook until the greens are wilted. Break the tomatoes into bite-size pieces and drop them into the pot, along with their juices. Add the broth, potatoes, lentils, lemon juice, thyme, and rosemary. Return the sausage to the pot.

3. Set the pressure cooker to high and cook for 18 minutes. Let the pressure release naturally for 10 minutes before opening. Serve the stew topped with grated Parmesan, if using.

Instant Pot Chicken Chili
Topped Your Way

MAKES 8 SERVINGS

2 tablespoons extra-virgin olive oil

1 large onion, chopped

1 large green bell pepper, chopped

4 garlic cloves, sliced

2 chipotle chiles (from a can of chipotle chiles in adobo sauce), chopped

1½ teaspoons ground cumin

1½ teaspoons kosher salt

1 teaspoon chili powder

1 (28-ounce) can whole tomatoes

1¾ cups (12 ounces) dry pinto beans, rinsed and picked over

½ cup tomato sauce

⅓ cup chopped fresh cilantro

1 pound boneless, skinless chicken breasts

3 cups (24 ounces) chicken broth

Toppings

Fresh or frozen and thawed corn kernels

Sour cream

Lime wedges

Chopped fresh cilantro

Shredded Pepper Jack cheese

Sliced black olives

Sliced fresh or pickled jalapeños

Chopped red onions

Tortilla chips

This spicy chili studded with chipotle chiles and pinto beans is tasty as is. But there's more to it than what's in the pot. This recipe is also equipped to conquer a crowd of eaters with different tastes. How so? While it cooks, you prep a mini buffet of toppings and put them in individual ramekins. Once the chili is ladled into bowls, everyone gets to add in what they like, salad bar–style. Think of it as no-whining dining.

1. Set an electric pressure cooker to sauté and warm the oil. Add the onion and bell pepper, and cook until they begin to soften, about 3 minutes. Add the garlic, chiles, cumin, salt, and chili powder, and cook until fragrant, 1 minute. Add the tomatoes, crushing them into pieces with your hands, along with their juices. Stir in the beans, tomato sauce, and cilantro, then slide in the chicken and cover with the broth.

2. Use a wooden spoon to press all the ingredients beneath the broth. Seal the pot and cook at high pressure for 50 minutes. (As it cooks, prep the toppings you plan to use and place them in bowls.) Let the pressure release naturally for 10 minutes before opening. Use a wooden spoon to break the chicken into pieces, then stir the soup to blend evenly. Serve immediately with your desired toppings.

Instant Pot Chicken Chili
Topped Your Way (page 50)

Root Vegetable Latkes
with Romesco Sauce

**MAKES 12 LATKES AND
ROMESCO SAUCE**

Romesco Sauce

2 whole roasted red bell
peppers

3 whole plum tomatoes (from
a 14-ounce can)

¼ cup whole almonds, toasted

2 tablespoons sherry vinegar

2 teaspoons smoked paprika

1¼ teaspoons kosher salt

¼ teaspoon freshly ground
black pepper

1 garlic clove, smashed

½ cup extra-virgin olive oil

Latkes

1 large russet potato, peeled
and grated

1 large onion, grated

2 large carrots, peeled and
grated

1 medium turnip, grated

⅓ cup all-purpose flour

2 teaspoons kosher salt

½ teaspoon freshly ground
black pepper

1 egg

Vegetable oil, for frying

*It's not an exaggeration to say that I am deeply
infatuated with romesco sauce. It's just so dang
delicious—garlicky and smoky with rich texture and
umami flavor from a blend of tomatoes and roasted red
bell peppers. It's paired here with panfried latkes made
with a combination of potatoes, turnips, and carrots—
more turnip-y than potato-y. You'll have plenty of the
sauce left over to use elsewhere, though you shouldn't
expect it to last long.*

1. To make the romesco sauce, combine the bell peppers,
tomatoes, almonds, vinegar, paprika, salt, black pepper,
and garlic in a food processor. Pulse several times to blend.
With the processor running, slowly stream in the olive oil
and process until smooth and creamy. Taste and adjust the
seasoning if needed. Transfer to a bowl and set aside.

2. To make the latkes, place the grated potato, onion,
carrots, and turnip in a large colander. Press the vegetables
against the sides of the colander to squeeze out the excess
liquid. Transfer to a medium bowl and stir in the flour, salt,
pepper, and egg.

3. Heat ¼ inch of vegetable oil in a large high-sided skillet
over medium-high heat. Line a plate with paper towels.
Scoop a 2-tablespoon portion of the potato mixture and
place it in the pan. Flatten it gently with the back of a spatula. Repeat, adding a few more mounds, but being careful
not to overcrowd the skillet.

4. Cook the latkes until they are golden brown, 3 to 4 minutes per side. Drain on the prepared plate. Repeat with the
remaining potato mixture. Serve the latkes immediately,
with the romesco sauce on the side.

Spaghetti with Pan-Roasted Cauliflower
and No-Cook Tomato Sauce

MAKES 6 SERVINGS

- 3 tablespoons extra-virgin olive oil
- 2 garlic cloves, sliced
- ⅓ cup panko breadcrumbs
- Kosher salt
- Freshly ground black pepper
- 10 ounces spaghetti
- 2 tablespoons unsalted butter
- 1 medium head cauliflower (any color), cut into large florets
- 2 cups No-Cook Tomato Sauce (page 92), at room temperature
- Parsley leaves, for garnish (optional)

If you're a fan of oven-roasted cauliflower, you'll appreciate the golden results of this stovetop method. The florets are browned in a pan with butter and oil, then scattered over a bed of noodles and topped with fresh and saucy No-Cook Tomato Sauce (page 92) and crunchy garlic breadcrumbs. It's a summery, satisfying meal bursting with delectable taste and texture.

1. Warm 1 tablespoon of the oil and the garlic in a large nonstick pan over medium heat. Sauté, stirring frequently, until the garlic begins to sizzle. Add the breadcrumbs and toast until golden, about 5 minutes. Season with salt and pepper and transfer to a small bowl. Set aside. Wipe the pan clean with a paper towel.

2. Bring a large pot of salted water to a boil. Add the spaghetti and cook according to the package directions.

3. While the pasta cooks, place 1 tablespoon of the remaining oil and 1 tablespoon of the butter in the pan over medium-low heat. Once the butter has melted, add half the cauliflower and cook, undisturbed, until golden brown on one side, about 4 minutes. Flip and cook on the other side, about 3 minutes. Transfer to a plate, then repeat with the remaining oil, butter, and cauliflower.

4. Spread the pasta on a large platter. Top with the cauliflower and the tomato sauce. Garnish with the breadcrumbs and parsley, if using. Serve immediately.

Creamy Garlic Pasta
with Ricotta and Sun-Dried Tomatoes

MAKES 4–6 SERVINGS

- 12 ounces rigatoni
- 1 cup whole milk ricotta
- ½ teaspoon lemon zest
- 1¼ teaspoons kosher salt
- ¼ teaspoon freshly ground black pepper
- 2 tablespoons extra-virgin olive oil
- 6 garlic cloves, sliced
- ½ cup sun-dried tomatoes in oil, drained, rinsed, and finely chopped
- Red pepper flakes
- 5 cups fresh baby spinach
- Grated Parmesan cheese, for serving

There's a trick to making a good creamy sauce, and it's not your choice of ingredients. Heat plays a big role in making or (literally) breaking a sauce's silky texture. Enter ricotta! It holds up to heat, and its subtle flavor is a great vehicle for other ingredients (here, it's lemon). Don't forget to reserve some pasta water to add in the final step so the dish turns out creamy rather than clumpy.

1. Bring a large pot of salted water to a boil. Add the rigatoni and cook according to the package directions. Drain, reserving ½ cup of the pasta water.

2. While the pasta cooks, stir together the ricotta, lemon zest, 1 teaspoon of the salt, and the pepper in a small bowl. Set aside.

3. Warm the oil in a large skillet over medium heat. Add the garlic and cook until fragrant, 1 minute. Stir in the tomatoes, 2 generous pinches of pepper flakes, the spinach, and the remaining ¼ teaspoon salt. Cook until the spinach is wilted, about 3 minutes. Add the cooked pasta and toss for 2 minutes to warm through.

4. Transfer the pasta to a serving bowl and add the ricotta mixture, along with 2 tablespoons of the reserved pasta water. Toss until the pasta is well coated. If the sauce is too thick, add more water, 1 tablespoon at a time. Serve immediately, with grated Parmesan on the side.

Ravioli Lasagna
with Any-Day Red Sauce

MAKES 6–8 SERVINGS

- 2 tablespoons extra-virgin olive oil
- 4 garlic cloves, sliced
- 2 (5-ounce) bags fresh baby spinach, roughly chopped
- Kosher salt and freshly ground black pepper
- 2½ cups Any-Day Red Sauce (page 95)
- 3 (9-ounce) packages fresh cheese ravioli
- 6 ounces fresh mozzarella, thinly sliced
- 2 tablespoons chopped basil leaves

There's no question about it: Eating lasagna is far more enjoyable than making it. Part of that (for me at least) has to do with all the time-consuming assembly. Using ravioli eliminates the need for layering the pasta and cheese, so the dish comes together quickly. I can't take credit for this genius idea, but I can assure you it's a legitimately tasty way to make your next pan.

1. Preheat the oven to 400°F (200°C).

2. Warm the oil in a large skillet over medium heat. Add the garlic and cook until fragrant, 1 minute. Add the spinach a few handfuls at a time, stirring frequently and letting it cook down slightly between additions. Season with salt and pepper, then continue to sauté until the spinach wilts completely. Let cool slightly, then transfer the spinach to a colander and use your hands or the back of a spoon to press and squeeze out the excess moisture.

3. Spread ⅓ cup of the sauce over the bottom of an 8-inch square baking dish. Add one-third of the ravioli in a single layer, then top with one-third each of the spinach and sauce. Scatter on one-third of the mozzarella. Repeat the layers twice more, beginning each with the ravioli and ending with the cheese.

4. Cover the baking dish tightly with foil and bake for 30 minutes. Uncover, then bake for about 20 minutes longer, or until bubbly and lightly browned. Let the lasagna rest for 10 minutes. Top with the basil before serving.

Pizza Margherita

MAKES 1 PIZZA

---

5 whole plum tomatoes
(from a 14-ounce can)

1 garlic clove, grated

Freshly ground black
pepper

Kosher salt (optional)

Cornmeal, for dusting

1 pound pizza dough
(choose your favorite)

8 ounces fresh mozzarella,
thinly sliced

1 tablespoon extra-virgin
olive oil, plus more for
drizzling

8 basil leaves, chopped

Believe it or not, a quick raw sauce made from canned plum tomatoes can be just as good (if not better) than store-bought pizza sauce. It's especially great on this Italian-style pie that's also topped with fresh mozzarella and basil. If your pizza is well baked, but you'd like a little more char, place it under the broiler for a minute or two. Just keep a close watch so it doesn't burn.

1. Preheat the oven to 500°F (260°C).

2. Add the tomatoes to a small bowl, and use your hands to crush them into bite-size pieces. Stir in the garlic and season to taste with pepper and, if needed, salt.

3. Sprinkle a baking sheet with cornmeal. Stretch the dough onto a 12-inch round pan, then spread on the tomato sauce, leaving a 1-inch border. Arrange the mozzarella on top. Brush the crust with the oil.

4. Bake the pizza for about 15 minutes, or until the cheese is melted and bubbly and the crust is charred in spots. Drizzle with oil and scatter on the basil just before serving.

Fall Vegetable Curry

MAKES 6 SERVINGS

Canola oil

1 (14-ounce) block extra-firm tofu, drained, pressed, and cut into 1-inch cubes

1 tablespoon Thai green curry paste

1 medium red bell pepper, sliced into thin strips

½ medium butternut squash, peeled and cut into 1-inch cubes (about 3 cups)

2 cups cauliflower florets

6 Campari tomatoes, squeezed and roughly chopped

½ teaspoon kosher salt

1 (14-ounce) can coconut milk

⅓ cup chicken broth

1 tablespoon lime juice

1 tablespoon fish sauce

1 tablespoon firmly packed brown sugar

¼ cup roughly chopped Thai basil leaves, plus more for garnish

Cooked rice, for serving

This dish is inspired by Thai green curry, but it's not at all authentic. It begins with a sauce made with spicy green curry paste, coconut milk, and lime. A flavorful matchup of butternut squash, cauliflower, and bell pepper lends a little sweetness. If you're fearless when it comes to heat, you can add an extra teaspoon or two of curry paste.

1. Heat ½ inch of oil in a large high-sided skillet over medium-high heat. Line a plate with paper towels. Working in batches, panfry the tofu, flipping occasionally, until golden on all sides, about 3 minutes per side. Drain on the prepared plate.

2. Warm 1 tablespoon oil in a large pot over medium-high heat. Stir in the curry paste and cook until fragrant, about 1 minute. Add the bell pepper and cook for 2 minutes. Add the squash, cauliflower, and tomatoes, and season with the salt. Stir to coat. Add the coconut milk, broth, lime juice, fish sauce, brown sugar, and half the basil. Press down the vegetables so they're covered by the sauce. Bring to a boil, then reduce to a simmer and cook, covered, stirring occasionally, for 20 minutes.

3. Stir in the tofu. Continue to cook, uncovered, stirring occasionally, until the vegetables are tender, about 10 minutes longer. Remove from the heat and stir in the remaining basil. Garnish with more basil and serve immediately with rice.

Grilled Cilantro-Basil Chicken Skewers
with Orzo Pilaf

MAKES 6 SERVINGS

Pilaf

2 tablespoons unsalted butter

¼ cup orzo

1½ cups long-grain white rice

2½ cups water

Kosher salt

Marinade

2 cups basil leaves

¾ cup cilantro leaves and tender stems

½ cup vegetable oil

2 garlic cloves, roughly chopped

1 teaspoon lime zest

2 tablespoons lime juice

1 small shallot, roughly chopped

½ teaspoon kosher salt

¼ teaspoon freshly ground black pepper

Chicken Skewers

1½ pounds boneless, skinless chicken thighs, cut into 1½- to 2-inch pieces

2 large zucchini, sliced into ¾-inch-thick half-moons

18 ounces cherry tomatoes

Kosher salt and freshly ground black pepper

2 tablespoons vegetable oil, for oiling the grates

Fresh cilantro and lime perk up the pesto-inspired marinade used to baste these chicken skewers. To get the end result good and saucy, half goes on before the skewers are cooked, then more is brushed on just before they come off the grill. The buttery pilaf served on the side is a nice complement to the charred chicken and veggies, and it's one of my go-to sides all summer long. For best results, soak twelve 9- or 10-inch bamboo skewers for 30 minutes before assembling the kebabs.

1. To make the pilaf, heat the butter in a saucepan over medium-high heat. Add the orzo and sauté, stirring frequently, until it begins to turn color slightly, about 2 minutes. Add the rice and sauté until the orzo is deep golden. Add the water, season with a few pinches of salt, and bring to a boil. Cover, reduce the heat to a simmer, and cook until the water is absorbed and the rice is tender, about 18 minutes. Remove from the heat.

2. Meanwhile, make the marinade. Combine the basil, cilantro, oil, garlic, lime zest, lime juice, shallot, salt, and black pepper in a food processor and pulse to finely chop the herbs, scraping down the sides as needed. Set aside half the marinade in a small bowl.

3. Preheat a gas or charcoal grill to medium-high heat.

4. To prepare the skewers, thread the chicken, zucchini, and tomatoes in an alternating pattern onto each skewer, then place the finished kebabs on a baking sheet. Brush them on all sides with the half portion of marinade still in the food processor. Season with salt and pepper.

5. Oil the grill grates. Place the kebabs on the grill and cook, turning occasionally, until charred in spots and the chicken is cooked through and no longer pink, 10 to 15 minutes total. Baste with the reserved marinade and grill for 2 minutes longer. Serve the kebabs immediately, with pilaf on the side.

Grilled Cilantro-Basil
Chicken Skewers
with Orzo Pilaf (page 66)

Baked Chicken Thighs
with Tomatoes, Olives, and Feta

MAKES 6 SERVINGS

- 4 sprigs oregano
- 4 sprigs thyme
- 6 bone-in, skin-on chicken thighs
- 3 cups cherry tomatoes
- 2 tablespoons extra-virgin olive oil
- 1¼ teaspoons kosher salt
- ¾ teaspoon freshly ground black pepper
- ¾ cup halved pitted Kalamata olives
- 4 garlic cloves, smashed
- 1 lemon, cut into wedges
- ½ cup crumbled feta cheese
- 2 tablespoons chopped fresh parsley

Boneless chicken thighs are great, but bone-in ones are even better. Cooking them on the bone results in juicier and more flavorful meat—not to mention a cheaper grocery bill. Rather than crisping the skin in a skillet before baking, this recipe relies on the broiler for the final step, which also gives the lemons and tomatoes a little char. It's a bit of a daredevil move, so keep watch to make sure the skin gets crispy, not burnt to a crisp.

1. Preheat the oven to 350°F (180°C).

2. Remove the leaves from the oregano and thyme sprigs and finely chop. Toss the chopped herbs together in a small bowl and set aside.

3. Place the chicken and tomatoes in a large roasting pan. Drizzle with the oil and toss to coat. Arrange in a single layer with the chicken skin-side up, then season with the salt and pepper. Scatter in the olives and tuck the garlic and lemon wedges around the chicken and tomatoes. Sprinkle the chopped oregano and thyme over the chicken.

4. Bake for 45 minutes. Baste the chicken with the pan juices, then bake for 20 minutes longer. Baste once more, then set the broiler to high and broil for 2 to 3 minutes, rotating the pan once, and keeping a close eye to prevent burning. Sprinkle on the feta and parsley just before serving with the pan juices.

Chicken Meatballs

with Any-Day Red Sauce

MAKES ABOUT 20 MEATBALLS

1½ pounds ground chicken (preferably a mix of light and dark meat)

1 small onion, finely chopped

¾ cup panko breadcrumbs

⅓ cup grated Parmesan cheese

1 garlic clove, grated

1 tablespoon chopped fresh parsley

2 teaspoons chopped fresh oregano

2 eggs

¾ teaspoon kosher salt

¼ teaspoon freshly ground black pepper

1 batch Any-Day Red Sauce (page 95), warmed, for serving

1 loaf crusty bread or baguette or ¾ pound cooked pasta, for serving (optional)

Meatballs made with poultry can often be dry, but they don't have to be. Opting for ground meat that's a blend of light and dark (found in most packaged offerings), or using just the latter, is a good start in the right direction. And adding ingredients like eggs and cheese provides extra moisture. Toss it all together with some fresh oregano and parsley and you've got yourself a nice, tender batch. Eat them with a slice of garlic bread, on a bun, or on top of your favorite pasta.

1. Line a baking sheet with foil. Position an oven rack 6 inches from the heat and preheat the broiler on high.

2. Combine the chicken, onion, breadcrumbs, Parmesan, garlic, parsley, oregano, eggs, salt, and pepper in a large bowl. Toss with your hands until evenly blended. Do not overmix.

3. Use your hands to shape the mixture into golf ball–size meatballs. Arrange on the prepared baking sheet, spacing them ½ inch apart.

4. Broil the meatballs for 4 minutes. Flip and broil for about 4 minutes longer, or until cooked through. Serve immediately with the tomato sauce and, if you like, bread or pasta.

Balsamic Grilled Flank Steak
with Tomatoes

MAKES 6 SERVINGS

- ¼ cup extra-virgin olive oil, plus more for grilling
- 3 tablespoons balsamic vinegar, plus more for drizzling
- 2 tablespoons lime juice
- 1 teaspoon honey
- 1 small garlic clove, grated

  Kosher salt and freshly ground black pepper
- 1½ pounds flank steak
- 5 firm, sweet, medium-size tomatoes (such as vine), halved crosswise
- 1 large red onion, cut into ½-inch-wide wedges

Flank steak requires little (if any) embellishment. But soaking in a marinade made with sweet and tangy balsamic vinegar, lime, and honey adds dimension to an already amazing cut. It's a quick cook on the grill, and you can make the vegetables while the meat rests. To keep the onions together while they cook, slice them into wedges with the root end still intact on the tip of each piece so the layers can't fall apart.

1. Whisk together the oil, vinegar, lime juice, honey, garlic, ¾ teaspoon salt, and ¼ teaspoon pepper in a large rectangular baking dish. Add the steak and turn to coat. Marinate in the refrigerator, turning once or twice, for at least 2 hours.

2. Preheat a gas or charcoal grill to high heat. Arrange the tomatoes and onion on a large baking sheet. Brush generously with oil and season with salt and pepper.

3. Oil the grill grates. Grill the steak until its internal temperature reaches 135°F (57°C) on an instant-read thermometer, about 6 minutes per side. Transfer to a cutting board and let rest.

4. Meanwhile, place the tomatoes and onion on the grill and cook until softened and charred, flipping halfway through, about 2 minutes per side. Set on a platter.

5. Slice the steak against the grain and place on top of the vegetables. Drizzle lightly with vinegar. Serve immediately.

Enchilada Stacks
with Chipotle Salsa

MAKES 4 SERVINGS

- 3 cups shredded chicken (from a rotisserie chicken)
- 1 (14-ounce) can pinto beans, drained and rinsed
- 3 scallions, minced
- ½ cup chopped fresh cilantro, plus more for garnish
- 12 (5- to 6-inch) corn tortillas
- ¾ cup Chipotle Salsa (page 29)
- 1½ cups shredded Mexican cheese blend

Using a rotisserie chicken to make dinner is a much-needed, tasty strategy that can help you add more variety to your day-to-day cooking. These stacks combine the chicken with pinto beans, cilantro, cheese, and homemade Chipotle Salsa (page 29) into an easy midweek meal (even if you wait until the day of to make the salsa). It's worth noting that each stack is really big and, depending on your appetite, potentially too much for one person. But that just means leftovers and less time in the kitchen the next day.

1. Preheat the oven to 375°F (190°C).

2. Combine the chicken, beans, scallions, and cilantro in a large bowl.

3. Arrange 4 tortillas on a baking sheet. Cover each with 1 tablespoon of the salsa, and top each with ½ cup of the chicken mixture followed by 2 tablespoons of the cheese. Top each with a tortilla. Repeat the layers, starting with salsa and ending with another tortilla. Spread one-quarter of the remaining salsa atop each stack, then sprinkle each with the remaining cheese.

4. Bake the stacks for 15 to 20 minutes, or until the edges of the tortillas are golden and the cheese is melted. Remove from the oven and garnish with more cilantro. Serve immediately.

Oven-Baked Cod

with Dill and Sungold Cherry Tomatoes

MAKES 4 SERVINGS

3 tablespoons unsalted
  butter, softened

1 garlic clove, grated

1 tablespoon chopped fresh
  dill, plus more for garnish

  Kosher salt and freshly
  ground black pepper

4 (4- to 6-ounce) cod fillets

1½ cups halved Sungold cherry
  tomatoes

1 small lemon, thinly sliced

The classic French cooking method called en
papillote—*a fancy way of saying putting food in a
packet and baking it with steam—is a quick, incredibly
easy, and nearly foolproof technique for preparing fish.
To do it, the fish is seasoned and layered with aromatics,
then wrapped in parchment paper and placed in the
oven. You can make it into a meal by adding quick-
cooking vegetables like (surprise!) the tomatoes in this
recipe. For the best results, portion your ingredients
evenly so all the packets are ready at the same time.*

1. Preheat the oven to 400°F (200°C). Cut four 12-inch
squares of parchment paper.

2. Stir together the butter, garlic, dill, ¾ teaspoon salt, and
¼ teaspoon pepper in a small bowl.

3. Arrange a fillet in the center of each parchment
sheet and season with salt and pepper. Dot each fillet
with one-quarter of the compound butter. Evenly divide
the tomatoes among the packets and top each with
1 or 2 lemon slices.

4. Fold or twist each sheet of parchment to seal in the
ingredients. Arrange the packets on a baking sheet. Bake
the fish for about 12 minutes, or until it is no longer opaque.
Garnish with more dill before serving.

BBQ Pulled Pork Sliders

with Sweet, Spicy, Smoky Barbecue Sauce

MAKES 6 SERVINGS

- 1 (6-pound) bone-in pork shoulder (I prefer a bone-in picnic shoulder)
- Kosher salt and freshly ground black pepper
- 1 large onion, halved and sliced
- ½ cup water
- 1 cup Sweet, Spicy, Smoky Barbeque Sauce (page 96), plus more for serving
- 12 mini pull-apart slider buns or dinner rolls (don't pull them apart!)
- 24 pickle slices

If you've ever made pulled pork in a slow cooker, you know it's an all-day affair. But on the up side, there's nothing quite like the tender end result, served best with a slathering of barbecue sauce. The recipe here yields just one batch of sliders—cleverly assembled using pull-apart buns or rolls so you only have to make one giant sandwich—but you'll have enough pork for two batches. If you'd like to double the sliders, use eight cups of cooked pork and twice the amount of sauce, pickles, and buns.

1. Generously season the pork shoulder with salt and pepper, then place it in a slow cooker skin-side up. Arrange the onion slices in a single layer on top and pour the water into the cooker. Cover and cook on low until an instant-read thermometer inserted in the thickest part registers 185°F (85°C), about 8 hours. The meat should be tender and falling off the bone. Reserve 1 tablespoon of the drippings.

2. Let the meat cool slightly, then transfer to a cutting board and shred. Place 4 cups of the meat in a bowl and stir in the barbecue sauce, along with the reserved drippings.

3. Position an oven rack 6 inches from the heat. Preheat the broiler.

4. Horizontally slice the buns, keeping each half intact so there are two large pieces. Arrange the halves cut-side up on a baking sheet. Toast under the broiler for about 2 minutes, or until golden, keeping close watch so they don't burn.

5. Spoon the pork on the bottom half of the buns. Scatter on the pickles, then cover with the bun tops. Serve immediately with extra barbecue sauce.

Worth-the-Wait Pot Roast

MAKES 6 SERVINGS

- 1 (3-pound) chuck roast
- Kosher salt and freshly ground black pepper
- 2 tablespoons extra-virgin olive oil
- 1 medium onion, chopped
- 4 garlic cloves, sliced
- 1 (28-ounce) can whole tomatoes
- ½ cup dry red wine
- 1½ cups beef broth
- 3 sprigs rosemary, plus more for garnish
- 3 sprigs thyme, plus more for garnish
- 1 pound baby potatoes
- 3 large carrots, peeled, halved, and cut into 2-inch pieces

Nearly every time I try to make pot roast, life stuff gets in the way, and I'm too hungry to wait or don't have enough hours to spare. But when I do manage to pull it off, it's a small victory and 100 percent worth it. Knowing the effort involved, this version includes carrots and potatoes so you don't have to make anything else (though a knob of bread would be nice, too). The vegetables soak up the braising liquid as they cook, which gives them tons of flavor.

1. Preheat the oven to 300°F (150°C).

2. Generously season the roast with salt and pepper. Heat the oil in a large Dutch oven over medium-high heat. Sear the roast on all sides until nicely browned, 2 to 3 minutes per side. Transfer to a large plate.

3. Add the onion to the pot and cook, stirring occasionally, until softened, about 3 minutes. Add the garlic and cook 1 minute. Add the tomatoes and their juices, breaking them up into small pieces with your hands. Pour in the wine. Use a wooden spoon to scrape up the browned bits from the bottom of the pot, then bring to a simmer and let cook until the liquid is slightly reduced, about 5 minutes.

4. Stir in the broth, rosemary, and thyme, then return the roast to the pot. Cover and bake for 1½ hours.

5. Add the potatoes and carrots to the pot, cover, and return to the oven. Bake for 1½ to 2 hours more, or until the vegetables are cooked through and the meat is tender. To serve, slice the meat, then arrange the vegetables on a platter and set the meat on top. Garnish with more rosemary and thyme.

Spicy Greens with Sausage, Farro, and Pickled Tomatoes

MAKES 5 SERVINGS

Pickled Tomatoes

- 1 large beefsteak tomato, seeded and chopped
- 1 small shallot, halved and thinly sliced
- 3 tablespoons white vinegar
- ½ teaspoon kosher salt

  Freshly ground black pepper

Greens and Sausage

- 2 tablespoons extra-virgin olive oil
- 5 uncooked hot Italian sausage links
- 1 medium onion, sliced
- 3 garlic cloves, sliced
- 1½ cups chicken broth
- 1 teaspoon kosher salt
- ¼ teaspoon freshly ground black pepper

  Red pepper flakes
- 2 pounds mustard greens (about 2 large or 3 small bunches), tough stems removed, roughly chopped

  Cooked farro, for serving

When a pot of collards arrived at my childhood dinner table, it was always accompanied by something my family called a "pickling plate"—a small platter of fresh tomatoes and onions to top the slow-braised greens. It never involved pickles, and I'm not even sure where the name came from, but the combination of fresh vegetables layered atop silky greens is one I haven't lost love for. It's the inspiration for this easygoing weeknight meal.

1. To make the pickled tomato, stir together the tomato, shallot, vinegar, salt, and a few grinds of black pepper in a small bowl. Set aside so the tomato pickles while you prepare the rest of the recipe.

2. To make the greens and sausage, warm the oil in a Dutch oven over medium heat. Add the sausages and brown on each side (they don't need to be cooked through at this point). Transfer to a plate. Add the onion and cook until softened, about 5 minutes. Add the garlic and cook for 1 minute. Add the broth, salt, black pepper, and a generous pinch of pepper flakes. Use a wooden spoon to scrape the browned bits from the bottom of the pot.

3. Stir in the greens, a few handfuls at a time, letting them wilt slightly between additions. Continue to stir until the greens completely wilt. Press the greens into the liquid (it's okay if they're not covered completely), then reduce the heat to a gentle simmer. Nestle the sausages on top of the greens, making sure they don't touch the bottom of the pot so they don't overcook. Cover and cook for 20 minutes.

4. Give the greens a stir, then reposition the lid so the pot is partially covered. Let the greens cook for 5 minutes longer. To serve, spoon a portion of farro onto each plate. Add a sausage link along with some greens and their juices. Top with pickled tomatoes.

Gingery Bacon-Tomato Fried Rice

MAKES 4 SERVINGS

- 4 strips bacon, thinly sliced crosswise
- 4 scallions, whites minced and green parts sliced
- 2 garlic cloves, minced
- 2 teaspoons minced fresh ginger
- 6 Campari tomatoes, squeezed and roughly chopped
- ½ cup frozen edamame, thawed
- 2 tablespoons soy sauce
- 1 tablespoon coconut aminos
- ½ teaspoon toasted sesame oil
- 3 eggs, lightly whisked
- 3 cups cooked brown rice

The main ingredients in this fried rice aren't exactly classic, but I can assure you, they work. Bacon is a no-brainer replacement for meatier bits of pork, and the tomatoes add an extra dose of umami that mingles well with everything else. Coconut aminos give the rice just a splash of sweetness that brings it all together into one good bowl.

1. Heat a large nonstick skillet over medium-high heat. Add the bacon and cook, stirring occasionally, until crisp, about 5 minutes. Stir in the scallion whites, garlic, and ginger, and cook until fragrant, about 1 minute. Add ½ cup of the tomatoes and cook until softened. Stir in the edamame, soy sauce, coconut aminos, and oil, and cook for 1 minute.

2. Push the mixture to the side of the skillet, pour in the eggs, and scramble until cooked through, about 2 minutes. Add the rice and continue to cook, stirring often, until well blended, about 2 minutes. Stir in the remaining tomatoes and cook until until warmed through. Serve immediately, topped with the scallion greens.

Tomato Vinaigrette

MAKES 1 CUP

1 sweet, ripe medium-size red tomato, roughly chopped

2 tablespoons white balsamic vinegar

1 tablespoon roughly chopped shallot

1 teaspoon Dijon mustard

1 garlic clove, roughly chopped

1½ teaspoons kosher salt

¼ teaspoon freshly ground black pepper

¼ cup extra-virgin olive oil

My pantry is filled with all sorts of vinegars, and white balsamic is one of my favorites. It's similar to dark balsamic but has a mellower flavor that's less overpowering. I like to use it in dressings and dishes where I want more of the other ingredients to shine through. It's perfect for this vinaigrette, where its acidic quality complements the fresh tomato. The dressing is incredibly good as is, but, if your salad is a simpler one, you can blend in a couple tablespoons of chopped fresh dill for added dimension.

1. Place the tomato, vinegar, shallot, mustard, garlic, salt, and pepper in a blender and purée.

2. With the blender running, slowly pour in the oil until the dressing is emulsified. Taste and adjust the flavors as desired. Refrigerate until ready to use.

Herb-Roasted Grape Tomatoes

MAKES ABOUT 2 CUPS

2 pints grape or cherry tomatoes

1 tablespoon extra-virgin olive oil

4 sprigs thyme

¼ teaspoon kosher salt

Freshly ground black pepper

Oven-roasting tomatoes gives them flavorful dimension and brings out their sweetness. More than just a base for a soup (though there is a good one on page 46) or sauce, you can toss them in salads, stir them into a warm pot of grains, or use them with hummus or cheese to make a simple crostini. I like to pair them with thyme, but rosemary and oregano— or a combination of herbs—will work, too.

1. Preheat the oven to 425°F (220°C).

2. On a large rimmed baking sheet, toss together the tomatoes, oil, thyme, salt, and a generous pinch of pepper. Roast for about 20 minutes, giving the pan a good shake halfway through, until the tomatoes have wrinkled slightly and are brown in spots.

3. Remove and discard the thyme sprigs. Serve warm or at room temperature.

BASICS

No-Cook Tomato Sauce

1 pound (about 2 medium-size) heirloom tomatoes, seeded and roughly chopped

½ pound sweet, small tomatoes, such as cherry or Campari, squeezed and finely chopped

2 garlic cloves, grated

¼ cup extra-virgin olive oil

Red pepper flakes

¾ teaspoon kosher salt

½ teaspoon freshly ground black pepper

2 tablespoons chopped fresh parsley

2 tablespoons chopped basil leaves

This super fresh sauce is a great way to use the summer's sweetest tomatoes without having to cook them. The longest step in making it is the wait to let the flavors meld. Use it simply to top a bowl of your favorite pasta, or take it up a notch and make the Spaghetti with Pan-Roasted Cauliflower and No-Cook Tomato Sauce (page 56). It takes only a few extra minutes, and the payoff is crazy delicious.

1. In a large bowl, stir together the tomatoes, garlic, oil, a pinch of pepper flakes, salt, and black pepper. Let sit at room temperature for 1 hour so the flavors meld.

2. Stir in the parsley and basil.

Any-Day Red Sauce

MAKES ABOUT 5½ CUPS

- 2 tablespoons extra-virgin olive oil
- 1 large onion, chopped
- 4 garlic cloves, thinly sliced
- 2 (28-ounce) cans whole tomatoes
- 3 sprigs oregano
- 2 sprigs rosemary
- 2 teaspoons kosher salt
- ¾ teaspoon freshly ground black pepper
- 2 tablespoons unsalted butter

Ripe, sauce-worthy tomatoes can be hard to come by beyond the summer months. This sauce relies on canned tomatoes so you can enjoy it all year round. At my house, where there's always something new simmering on the stove, this is one of the few back-pocket recipes that stays in rotation. The sauce is quick enough to pull off on a weeknight (really!) and so much better than anything you can buy. A bit of butter adds richness. Just toss with your favorite pasta.

1. Warm the oil in a large high-sided skillet or Dutch oven over medium heat. Add the onion and cook until softened, about 3 minutes. Add the garlic and cook for 1 minute.

2. Use your hands to break the tomatoes into small pieces and add them, along with their juices, to the skillet. Stir in the oregano and rosemary, and season with the salt and pepper. Bring to a simmer, then lower the heat and cook, stirring occasionally, until thickened and saucy, about 30 minutes.

3. Remove the herb stems from the sauce (most of the leaves will come off during cooking), turn off the heat, and stir in the butter. Serve immediately. Can be refrigerated for up to 3 days.

Sweet, Spicy, Smoky Barbecue Sauce

BASICS

MAKES ABOUT 2½ CUPS

2 cups ketchup (I prefer Heinz)

1½ cups cider vinegar

¾ cup firmly packed dark brown sugar

¼ cup plus 2 tablespoons molasses

2 large garlic cloves, smashed

1¼ teaspoons lemon zest

2 tablespoons lemon juice

1 tablespoon liquid smoke

2 teaspoons smoked paprika

1¼ teaspoons kosher salt

1 teaspoon freshly ground black pepper

1 teaspoon red pepper flakes

I come from a line of incredible barbecue masters and have tried for years to replicate the sauce my mother makes, which is nothing short of legendary. But after endless tutorials in her kitchen and hours spent trying to decode measurements like "Until it tastes right," and, "I don't know how much . . . some," I've decided to make it my own way. While admittedly my mom's sauce will always be better, this version is inspired by what makes hers worthy of bartering for, as her neighbors constantly do—a nice balance of sugar, spice, and smoke.

1. Place the ketchup and vinegar in a saucepan over high heat. Whisk together until smooth. Add the sugar and molasses, and stir until dissolved. Stir in the garlic, lemon zest, lemon juice, liquid smoke, paprika, salt, black pepper, and pepper flakes.

2. Bring the mixture to a boil, then reduce to a simmer. Cover and cook until reduced by one-third, about 45 minutes. Let cool, then refrigerate until ready to use.

ACKNOWLEDGMENTS

Many hands went into shaping this book, and I am grateful for every human who lent theirs—most especially because a lot of it happened during the height of the pandemic, a time that felt uncertain and often frightening. Thanks first to the team at Storey Publishing, including acquisitions editor Deanna Cook, who planted the seed for this project one sunny, socially distanced afternoon on her front porch with a cup of tea and lots of ideas and encouragement. The keen eye and adept wordsmithing of my editor Sarah Guare are everything an author could hope for. Thank you! I also owe a debt of gratitude to the design work and visual guidance of Michaela Jebb, Liseann Karandisecky, Ian O'Neill, and Carolyn Eckert, who made this book a beauty. A shout-out also to Emma Sector, Paula Brisco, and Dan Cohen.

To the photo team, thank you for helping me bring life and order to all the chaotic creative ideas swirling in my head. Photographer Joe St. Pierre, you are a wonder, and working with you is always a gift. This time was no different! Prop stylist Ann Lewis, your incredible talent and commitment to this project meant more than I can express in this sentence. Thank you for all you do. And my #1, Laura Manning, there would be no photos in this book without you. I am eternally grateful for your friendship, wit, and the unabashed joy you bring to the kitchen. Thanks, too, to Julie Bozzo Cote and Jodi Villani for their generosity.

Recipe testers Laurel Brandstetter, Dave Butts, Ryan Cline, Jordan DeFrank, Christian Gregory, Krista Hojnowski, Rey Pamatmat, Carol Sellers, and Nicky Sumorok—your input made the book better than it would have ever been without you. Jessica and Salem Salloom, I owe you big-time for letting me turn a little corner of your house into my personal office space. Having a quiet place to sit with my thoughts and write is likely the only reason I was able to meet my deadlines. Debra Immergut, Betty Rosbottom, Sally Ekus, Lisa Ekus, and so many other colleagues and editors I've worked with—past and present—have given me an endless amount of good advice and direction. I appreciate you all! Jan and Patrice Sabach, your friendship and company was an incredibly bright beacon during a tumultuous and challenging time known as the year 2020. Nordic life forever!

And to my family: Mom and Dad, thanks for instilling in me a love for all things food (and drink!) related. It's because of you that I find myself here. "Brother" Les, you are THE best. Thank you for cheering me on literally every time we talk. Andiyah, Inez, and Zadie—spending time in the kitchen with each of you is one of my most favorite things, even if I have to wash all the dishes. And Chris, my person, thank you for eating copious amounts of tomatoes in and out of season with unwavering enthusiasm. You are my constant source of love and warmth. I still don't know how I got so lucky.

INDEX

Page numbers in *italics* indicate photographs.